Contents

the twelve steps

1 We admitted we were powerless over alcohol — that our lives had become unmanageable.

2 Came to believe that a Power greater than ourselves could restore us to sanity.

3 Made a decision to turn our will and our lives over to the care of God *as we understood Him.*

4 Made a searching and fearless moral inventory of ourselves.

5 Admitted to God, to ourselves, and to another human being the exact nature of our wrongs.

6 Were entirely ready to have God remove all these defects of character.

7 Humbly asked Him to remove our shortcomings.

8 Made a list of all persons we had harmed, and became willing to make amends to them all.

9 Made direct amends to such people whenever possible, except when to do so would injure them or others.

10 Continued to take personal inventory and when we were wrong promptly admitted it.

11 Sought through prayer and meditation to improve our conscious contact with God *as we understood Him,* praying only for knowledge of His will for us and the power to carry that out.

12 Having had a spiritual awakening as the result of these steps, we tried to carry this message to alcoholics, and to practice these principles in all our affairs.

What Is Chemical Dependence?

C hemical dependence is a disease that results in the compulsion to drink or use other drugs despite negative consequences. A chemically dependent person experiences a craving for a chemical. Chemicals can mean either alcohol or other mind-altering drugs. Chemical dependence affects the whole person — mind, feelings, body, values, and spirit.

For a chemically dependent person, the need for the chemical is always psychological but may be physical as well. Chemically dependent people use chemicals to feel good or avoid the discomfort of not using the chemical. As tolerance builds, the chemically dependent person must use more of the chemical to experience the "high" he or she is looking for.

Chemical dependence is often referred to as a disease of feelings. Often, chemically dependent people have grown up in families in which feelings were not openly expressed. Many never learned how to express feelings honestly and instead learned to hide or manipulate feelings.

"I don't smoke pot and drink to get high anymore. I do it just to get by."

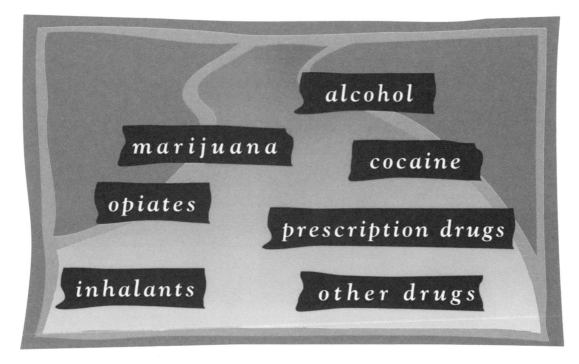

alcohol

marijuana

cocaine

opiates

prescription drugs

inhalants

other drugs

A chemical is a chemical is a chemical. To recover, chemically dependent people must abstain from all mind-altering drugs.

A Primary Disease

Chemical dependence is the primary disease — not the result of another problem. The disease of chemical dependence comes first: other consequences are caused by the dependence.

Physical consequences can include:

- Mental illness
- Heart disease
- Cancer
- Lung disease
- Malnutrition
- Hardening of the arteries

Social consequences can include:

- Dishonesty
- Loss of job
- Financial problems
- Spiritual loss
- Lying
- Family problems
- Hiding out

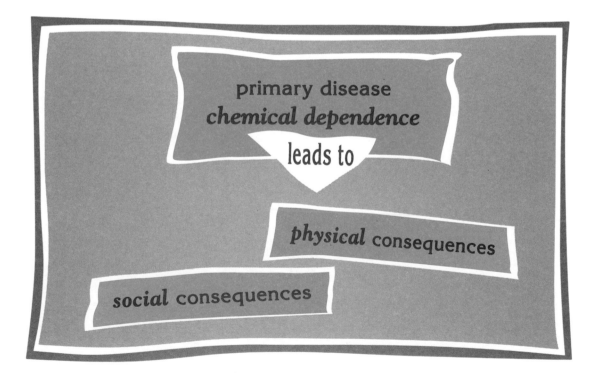

primary disease
chemical dependence
leads to

physical consequences

social consequences

By focusing on recovery from chemical dependence, we can start changing the consequences or problems that have resulted from our primary disease.

A Chronic, Progressive, Fatal Disease

Chronic

Chemical dependence is a chronic disease. It progresses slowly, is constant, and lasts for a long period of time. Other chronic diseases include diabetes and heart disease.

The disease of chemical dependence is slow and subtle. Chemically dependent people and those close to them may not be aware of the changes the disease causes in the dependent person, the family, and other relationships.

Progressive

The disease of chemical dependence is relentless. If left unchecked, the chemically dependent person moves from an early stage in which the chemical appears helpful and seductive to an uncontrollable craving.

In the late stages of the disease, the chemically dependent person's body starts to give up. Many physical problems arise. Mental, emotional, and spiritual strength is sapped. Problems become more severe over time.

Eventually Fatal

If the chemically dependent person continues to abuse alcohol or other drugs, the addiction will eventually lead to death due to:

- Liver, heart, kidney, pancreas, or lung failure
- Overdose
- Suicide
- Car, water, or fire-related accidents
- Violence

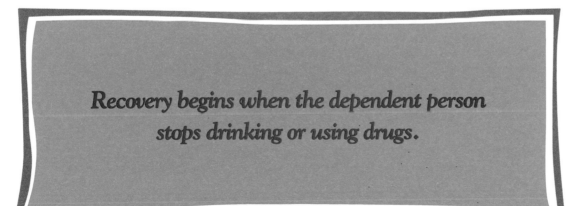

Recovery begins when the dependent person stops drinking or using drugs.

The Path to Addiction

Have you been on the path to addiction? Have you experienced problems caused by your use of alcohol or other drugs but been unable to change your behavior or use? Do you feel as if you move from one crisis to the next?

As chemically dependent people, we often do not connect our use of alcohol or other drugs with the problems which result from that use. For example, we might deny that our financial, family, health, or legal problems are a result of drinking or using chemicals.

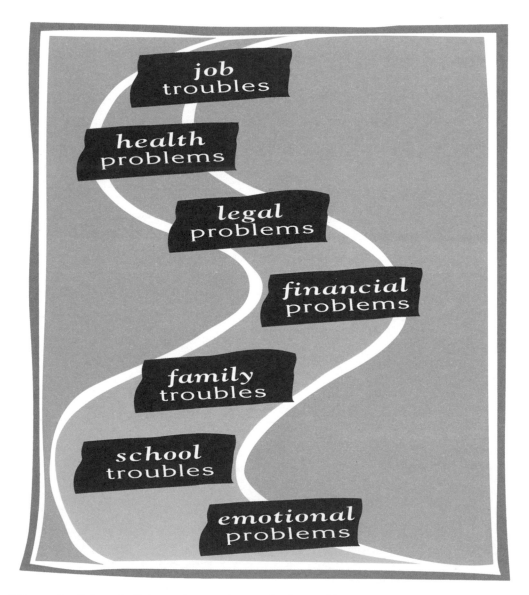

The path of chemical dependence often includes problems in various areas of our lives. Though we may not connect these problems with our chemical use, we may find in the process of recovery that these problems were the consequences of our use of alcohol or other drugs.

Describe the areas of your life that have been affected on your path to addiction.

How have you tried to change your behavior or chemical use?
Describe what happened.

Chemical Effects

A Drug I Have Abused: YES NO
(circle yes or no throughout)

How It Works

When you consume alcohol, 20 percent immediately passes through your stomach walls into the bloodstream. The remaining 80 percent goes to the small intestine where it slowly finds its way into your blood.

The body eliminates about one-half ounce of alcohol per hour (the same as one mixed drink, one beer, or one glass of wine).

If the average person drinks more rapidly, the alcohol content in the blood increases, and he or she experiences the intoxicating effects of the drug. Men and women break down alcohol at a different rate, so it's possible that a man and woman of the same weight will have different blood alcohol levels.

Damage Caused

Once alcohol enters the bloodstream, it enters all of your body's organs — brain, liver, heart, pancreas, kidneys, and lungs — within minutes.

When used over time, alcohol causes damage to liver, kidneys, pancreas, and lungs.

Pregnant women who continue to drink place the fetus at high risk for birth defects. Other physical and developmental problems may occur that can last a lifetime for the child. This is called Fetal Alcohol Syndrome (FAS).

In one hour, your body can eliminate about one-half ounce of alcohol. That's the same as one beer, one glass of wine, or one mixed drink.

Crack/Cocaine

A Drug I Have Abused: YES NO

How It Works

Cocaine is a powerful stimulant that creates a fast, intense high, a decrease in hunger, indifference to pain and fatigue, and illusions of great physical strength and mental capacity.

Crack is a condensed, highly concentrated form of cocaine. Therefore it is extremely addicting.

Damage Caused

Cocaine causes psychological problems including anxiety attacks, intense irritability, acute paranoia, hallucinations, violent behavior, and suicide.

Physical problems caused by cocaine use involve the brain, central nervous system, and heart. Cocaine causes dramatic changes in the way brain cells operate. As a powerful stimulant, it causes the activity of the brain to speed up. Cocaine use can result in violent seizures and death. Central nervous system damage may also occur.

Cocaine can kill through heart attacks. Heart attacks can be brought on by the extra strain forced on the heart when cocaine constricts blood vessels.

Cocaine can also cause death by suffocation. This can happen during an unnaturally deep sleep or unconsciousness. The numbed tissues in the back of the throat may block breathing. Cocaine is often mixed with other drugs, particularly alcohol, which greatly increases the user's risks.

Marijuana

A Drug I Have Abused: YES NO

How It Works

The marijuana smoked in the United States consists of the flower and dried leaves of the plant *cannabis sativa*.

Unlike alcohol, which is a simple chemical, marijuana contains over 400 chemicals, 60 of which are unique to the marijuana plant. Lighting marijuana causes formation of an additional 1,600 chemicals. As a pot smoker inhales, these chemicals invade every cell of the user's body.

The ingredient which creates marijuana's intoxication effect is Delta-9-THC, often referred to as THC.

Like alcohol, marijuana is a central nervous system depressant. And, like most other drugs, marijuana wears down the motivation of users. It erodes the will to perform. Ambition is lost. Success and achievement no longer matter to chronic marijuana users.

Damage Caused

In addition to the unknown short- and long-term dangers of so many chemicals entering the user's body, THC has a particular trait that increases its harmful effect:

- THC dissolves in fat, not in water.

Since the body rids itself of waste through a water system that includes urine, feces, sweat, and blood, THC cannot escape. It stays trapped in the body.

In addition, THC finds its resting place in fatty parts of the body. The most sensitive and critical are the:

- Brain
- Liver
- Lungs
- Reproductive system

Inhalants

Drugs I Have Abused:

How They Work

Inhalants are breathable chemicals that produce mind-altering vapors. Inhalants include amyl and butyl nitrate, solvents such as glue and lighter fluid, and aerosol products. They produce effects similar to anesthetics. Used in any amount, inhalants can cause physical damage, unconsciousness, and even death.

Damage Caused

Physically, inhalant use can cause nausea, lack of coordination, loss of appetite, slowed heart and breathing rates, and fatigue. Other damage can include weight loss, nervous system damage, and liver, kidney, blood, and bone damage.

Mentally, inhalant use can result in loss of self-control, violent behavior, losing touch with one's surroundings, and unconsciousness. Death from inhalant use is not unusual.

Opiates and Painkillers

Drugs I Have Abused: YES NO

How They Work

Opiates come from the juice in the unripe seed pods of the opium poppy. These drugs are used to relieve pain, coughing, and diarrhea. They also offer an intense high. Opiates give a brief, dream-like sense of well-being and relaxation. Their use results very quickly in addiction.

Heroin accounts for a large percentage of opiate abuse. However, medicines such as morphine, meperidine, and cough medicines with codeine are also abused and can lead to addiction.

Damage Caused

Side effects of opiate use include drowsiness, dizziness, constipation, euphoria, mood swings, and mental confusion. Over time, opiate users may develop infections of the heart lining and valves, skin problems, and congested lungs.

Hallucinogens

Drugs I Have Abused:

How They Work

Hallucinogens cause intense physical and psychological effects on the body and mind that alter perception, sensation, thinking, and feeling. Hallucinogens include drugs like LSD, mescaline, DMT, and peyote.

Damage Caused

Heavy users develop brain damage including poor memory and attention. Mood swings and impaired sense of time and self can cause panic. Mental or emotional problems that were not apparent before use can be unmasked with use of these drugs.

Prescription Drugs

Drugs I Have Abused: YES NO

How They Work

Prescription drugs pose a special danger for chemically dependent people. Often the abused prescription drugs are first taken for legitimate medical reasons. Dependence on prescription drugs can occur over a few weeks or several years. Denial, because of the nature of the initial use, can be very high. That is, if a doctor has prescribed a medication for a specific medical reason, many people simply don't believe that chemical dependence might occur.

When the chemically dependent person tries to stop using the prescription drug, the initial problem appears to re-emerge. New problems are often added. The addictive cycle starts over again. Recovering chemically dependent people must take responsibility for the prescription drugs they use. Use of such drugs must be monitored by a knowledgeable doctor. Use of any mind-altering drug can lead to relapse. We must tell the physician and/or pharmacist that we are chemically dependent. Careful monitoring of prescription drug use is important.

● Please complete the following for each drug you have used:

Drug	Age of first use	Age of last use	How much	How often	How used

● Has the amount of alcohol or drugs you need to use to get high changed over time? Describe.

_____

_____

_____

_____

_____

_____

_____

● Do you ever drink or use quickly to get high as soon as possible? _____

● Do you ever drink or use before a party or before an event? Describe.

_____

_____

_____

- Do you drink or use alone? _____

- Describe where and when. _____

_____

_____

_____

_____

_____

- Do you hide your alcohol or other drugs? _____

- Describe your hiding spots and explain why you hide your supply. _____

_____

_____

_____

_____

_____

- Have you ever passed out as a result of your chemical use? _____

- If so, how often? _____

_____

- Describe one such incident in detail. _____

_____

_____

_____

_____

● Do you have blackouts or times when you do not remember your actions? _____

Describe. _____

● Do you ever feel sick or overly nervous and shaky from your drinking or using? _____

Describe. _____

● Have you been warned by a doctor or other health worker about damage or possible damage to your body because of your use of chemicals? _____

Describe. _____

We admitted

we were

powerless

over

alcohol,

that our lives

had become

unmanageable.

The Beginning

I n this workbook you will learn about the first five Steps of Alcoholics Anonymous. The Twelve Steps have helped many people change their lives. Twelve Step programs work. They provide us with a different view of ourselves and others.

The Twelve Steps are the path to chemically free and sober living. The recovery path begins with taking the first Step. It's impossible to overestimate the importance of this Step. Until you are able to accept Step One, contented sobriety is not possible.

Acceptance

What makes acceptance so difficult? It's hard for any person to accept powerlessness and unmanageability. The task is even more difficult for chemically dependent people. Our judgment and behavior have been controlled for many years by alcohol or other drugs. We become defensive. Our ability to evaluate our own behavior has been destroyed. Feelings of shame, fear, and anger may further block the truth. Our ability to deny the results of our chemical use prevents us from drawing logical conclusions. (See page 22 for a discussion of denial.)

It is not surprising that we find defeat by chemicals difficult to accept.

Powerlessness

"So many mornings I would wake up and say to myself, `Today I will not take a drink or smoke a joint; today I will stay on track.' But by evening my hand was wrapped around a drink or I was lighting up."

As we develop a thorough understanding of our disease, we will begin to identify our personal powerlessness over alcohol and other drugs. The first part of Step One — we admitted we were powerless over our chemical dependence — asks us to understand how our chemical use controlled our behavior and actions.

What is powerlessness?
- When the urge to use alcohol or other drugs takes priority over the rest of your life, you are powerless.

- When any part of your family, health, work, or social life are put aside because of your chemical dependence, you are powerless.

- Whenever your chemical dependence interferes with your ability to manage your life — and you continue using — you are powerless.

It seems simple. Yet refusing to accept your own powerlessness may be the biggest roadblock to your recovery. By working at understanding and accepting your powerlessness, you will overcome that roadblock. You will remain on course on your journey to recovery.

● How has your use of alcohol and other drugs placed your life or others in danger?

● Give examples of how powerlessness has shown itself in your behavior.

● What does admitting powerlessness mean to you?

_____
_____
_____
_____
_____

● What does acceptance mean to you?

_____
_____
_____
_____
_____

● How are these two concepts different?

_____
_____
_____
_____
_____

● Are you admitting or accepting?

_____
_____
_____

● How is this shown in your behavior?

_____
_____
_____
_____

Attempts to Stop or Control

Often, chemically dependent people have recognized their need to stop using or drinking long before seeking help. Our excuses for using chemicals point out that recognition. For example, we might use excuses like these:

- I only drink after five o'clock.

- Complete abstinence from cocaine is the answer for me. But using marijuana or alcohol once in a while won't hurt.

- I only drink every other day.

- I'll only smoke marijuana on weekends.

- I only drink beer. It's not the same as hard liquor.

- If I only drink when I'm with other people, I'll be okay. No more drinking by myself.

- It's good discipline for me to stop drinking and using completely during the month of March.

- If I spend only $10 per week on alcohol, it won't be enough to cause me any problems.

- My weight is the real problem. So I'll quit drinking until I'm down to 120 pounds.

- I'll buy one bottle of scotch per week. That's all.

- I'll only do cocaine or crack on special occasions.

- I won't smoke pot in the morning.

Give examples of how you have tried to "control" your use of alcohol or other drugs.

Negative Consequences

Here are some examples of losses commonly experienced in the process of chemical dependence:

- a marriage
- a family relationship
- a friend or friends
- a job
- financial security
- good grades
- a professional opportunity
- an educational degree (high school, college, etc.)
- a driver's license or a professional license
- time (months or years)
- personal dignity and self respect
- a good credit rating
- the trust of others
- a house, car, or other property
- good health
- the health of loved ones

● List things your chemical dependence has caused you to lose.

How do you feel today about each of these negative consequences?

Loss of Control

Often, chemically dependent people do not plan to use or drink as much as they end up consuming. We lose control over the amount of alcohol or other drugs we take. This can cause us to behave in ways that are embarrassing or offensive. Often our behavior is in conflict with what we know is right.

Chemically dependent people vary greatly in patterns of use. Some drink or use daily, others only on weekends or even less often. What we have in common is a preoccupation with our drug of choice. We have given control over ourselves, our behavior, and our values to a chemical. The chemical has taken charge.

● Give specific examples of losing control. Describe how you lost your ability to stop drinking or using, and how your behavior went out of your control.

● Describe any abuse to yourself, family, or friends that occurred as a result of your alcohol or other drug use.

_____
_____
_____
_____
_____
_____
_____
_____

● What behavior of yours does your family or friends object to most?

_____
_____
_____
_____
_____
_____
_____

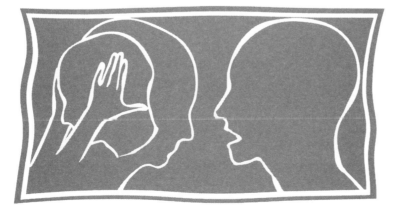

Denial

What Is Denial?

Denial is a way the mind handles the stress of having a long-lasting disease. People who deny become confused with what is true and what is false. They are unable to distinguish one from the other.

Chemically dependent people often continue to drink and use because they deny that they have a problem. At first, the denial may be just a spontaneous response to the problems that result from abusing chemicals. However, as more drugs are taken, the chemically dependent person loses his or her ability to accurately judge simple day-to-day situations. Some examples of denial include:

● People with heart disease who ignore warning signs and don't follow exercise and diet recommendations.

● People with diabetes who fail to make lifestyle changes that promote good health.

● Chemically dependent people who continue to use even despite harmful consequences.

How Denial Grows

This illustration shows how denial prevents us from acceptance. Denial works by piling one excuse on top of another. Denial causes confusion and leads us down the path to relapse rather than recovery.

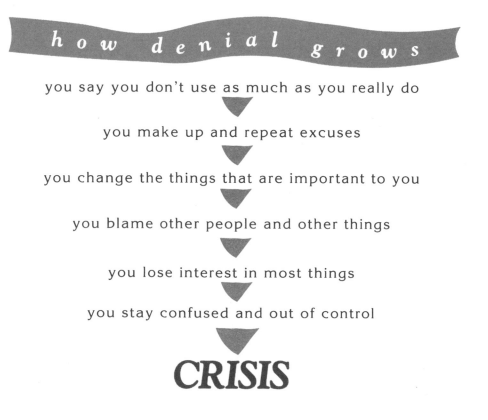

how denial grows

you say you don't use as much as you really do

▼

you make up and repeat excuses

▼

you change the things that are important to you

▼

you blame other people and other things

▼

you lose interest in most things

▼

you stay confused and out of control

▼

CRISIS

● How did you use denial in describing:

The amount you drank or used?

_____

_____

_____

_____

How often you drank or used?

_____

_____

_____

_____

The problems caused by your chemical use?

_____

_____

_____

_____

The harm you caused yourself or others by your behavior?

_____

_____

_____

_____

Listening and Accepting

As chemically dependent people we are not aware of our own twisting of the truth. By listening to others such as treatment peers, counselors, family members, and friends, we can learn important clues to our denial. But we must be willing to listen and accept what we hear.

As you break through one part of your denial, you may recognize other areas of denial more easily. Feel good about these discoveries. There is no reason to feel guilty. By breaking through denial, you have the knowledge to change. You have an accurate picture of yourself and the world around you. You are beginning your path to recovery.

Unmanageability

Unmanageability is related to powerlessness. It affects every area or our lives. It's impossible for those who are chemically dependent to keep functioning like healthy human beings. Things just don't seem to go smoothly. Areas of responsibility easily met by others are left in complete disorder by us, even when other people may pitch in and try to help. In fact, we often attempt to shift the blame onto other people.

As a result, we feel angry, resentful, fearful, and shameful. People around us become confused. They may respond in a manner that makes things even more unmanageable.

We may cling to one part of our lives (such as a job), while leaving other areas unattended. Many times we cannot see the unmanageable state of our affairs. The more we continue to drink or use to hide from the daily mess, the larger the mess becomes.

The First Step asks us to admit "that our lives had become unmanageable." When we begin to understand the ways in which our lives were out of control, we're taking the important first step on our journey to recovery.

What Does Unmanageability Mean to You?

The following questions will help you identify unmanageability in various areas of your life.

My Family and Friends

● Have you changed friends because of your drinking or using?_____

Describe._____

_____

_____

_____

_____

_____

● Give examples of your behavior that—because of your use of alcohol or other drugs—have caused problems with family or friends.

_____

● Has your relationship with your family changed due to your use of alcohol or other drugs?

Describe. _____

_____

Work/School

● Has your performance at work/school changed over time? _____

Describe. _____

_____

_____

_____

_____

_____

● Has your ability to think and remember been affected by your chemical use?

Give examples. _____

_____

_____

_____

_____

_____

_____

● Have you lost any opportunities because of your drinking or using?

Describe. _____

_____

_____

_____

_____

_____

● How would you evaluate your own work/school performance?

_____

_____

_____

_____

_____

_____

_____

Dangerous/Illegal Behavior

● Describe situations when you were (or could have been) arrested for illegal actions because of your use of alcohol or other drugs.

_____

_____

_____

_____

_____

_____

_____

_____

_____

_____

_____

_____

● Have you found yourself in dangerous situations because of alcohol or other drugs?_____

Describe. _____

_____
_____
_____
_____
_____
_____
_____
_____
_____
_____

● Have your actions while drunk or high caused you any physical harm (car accidents, falls, fires, fights, self-inflicted wounds)? _____

Describe._____

_____
_____
_____
_____
_____
_____
_____
_____
_____

Values

● Has drinking or using caused you to do things that go against your own values or caused you to become someone other than who you want to be? _____

Describe. _____

_____
_____
_____
_____
_____
_____
_____
_____
_____

Unmanageability Summary

Based on your responses to the questions above, answer the following:

Has your drinking or drug use made your life unmanageable? _____

Are you a chemically dependent person? _____

Do you wish to continue your recovery? _____

If so, give ten reasons why.

1. _____
2. _____
3. _____
4. _____
5. _____
6. _____
7. _____
8. _____
9. _____
10. _____

Spirituality, Chemical Dependence, and Recovery

Many chemically dependent people who enter treatment feel off track. We have lost track of our original values and beliefs. Our goals may have faded in the wake of our craving for alcohol or other drugs. The way we've spent our time may have left us feeling empty, alone, and frustrated.

Step Two asks us to translate those frustrations into a belief that if we can't bring our lives into clear focus, some Power outside of ourselves can. That Power could be a friend, a sponsor, or a Twelve Step support or recovery group. It could be a traditional belief in a God, or even the forces of nature.

Steps Two and Three often do not come quickly to recovering people. We fight and resist the word "sanity" (implying insanity), and the concept of a Higher Power. Many of us resist the idea of turning away from self-will to the will of a Higher Power.

Relax. The path of recovery is not a race. Just be open to new ways, new thoughts. Listen to others who have come to believe in a Higher Power. They have turned their will and lives over to that Higher Power.

● Have you felt off track?_____ If so, how?

● What does insanity or inappropriate behavior mean to you?

● Give examples of inappropriate behavior you showed while using chemicals.

● What does sanity or appropriate behavior mean to you?

● Give examples of how you show appropriate behavior.

Came to Believe

The first three words of the second Step are very important: "Came to believe." These words suggest that our spiritual discovery is a journey. We don't need to feel like we should have already arrived, or need to arrive by a certain time. Maybe you sense your journey has already begun. Fine. Maybe it is about to start. The important point is that you have a willingness.

●   Do you believe there is a power greater than yourself? _____

Explain. _____

A Power Greater Than Chemicals

Consider how important alcohol or other drugs have become to you. Did your chemical dependence control your thoughts and behavior? Can you think of alcohol or other drugs as a power that caused you to say and do things that went against your values and beliefs?

Here are examples of how chemical use can influence your attitudes and behavior:

- Nobody knows how hard life has been for me. No wonder I need to get high from time to time.

- My parents (spouse/teacher/co-worker/boss/friend) get in my way: I need to drink/use just to cope with them.

- It doesn't matter if I knowingly overspend.

- My husband (wife/partner) doesn't understand or appreciate me. I don't care what he or she thinks.

- I can drive just fine no matter how much I've had to drink (smoke/shoot/snort).

- I could do my job better if the boss would stay out of my hair.

- Who needs that kind of friend? He or she never did know how to have a good time.

- My kids don't listen to a thing I say, so why should I be held responsible for their behavior?

- I'm not being any more dishonest than everyone else.

Chemical dependence leaves us isolated from people and activities. The chemical takes on such importance that it breaks the ties we have with all that matters in our lives, including our Higher Power.

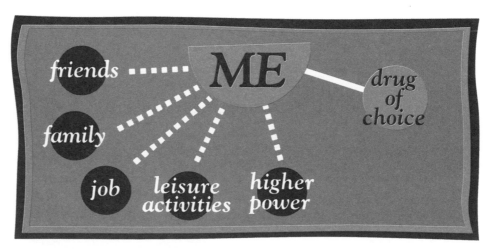

Chemical dependence binds us to our chemical while cutting us off from healthy sources of support.

Recovery allows us to link up once more to those people and activities that are important to us. Recovery allows us to regain a spiritual tie as well.

Recovery helps us connect with strong sources of support we need to maintain healthy sobriety.

● Have your ties to people or activities been altered or broken? _____

Describe. _____

_____

_____

_____

_____

● Which relationships or activities would you like to re-build in your life as part of your recovery? _____

_____

_____

_____

_____

Explain why. _____

_____

_____

_____

_____

_____

A Spiritual Journey

Spiritual growth is not an event but a journey. It continues throughout our lifetime. When our spiritual life is out of balance, everything else is out of balance as well.

A belief in a Higher Power rarely comes quickly. Faith is gained by taking small steps each day. The journey does not lead to an end called spiritual life. Instead, we experience many spiritual rewards along the path. The payoff comes in making the journey.

If you are not already on a spiritual journey, you can start today. This moment.

Write down the steps of your spiritual path using phrases from the list provided or other phrases you can think of. Your path does not need to be in any special order or have a definite beginning or end.

- Singing/dancing/music
- Enjoying quiet, solitude
- Asking for forgiveness
- Working
- Walking, exercising
- Smiling, laughing
- Reading, learning
- Helping others
- Sharing experiences

- Forgiving others
- Attending a church, synagogue or temple
- Appreciating nature
- Loving others unselfishly
- Listening to others
- Sharing feelings
- Remembering, reflecting
- Keeping a journal

Made a

decision

to turn

our will

and our

lives over

to the care of

God

as we

understood

Him.

Turning It Over

S tep Three brings us to a choice. If we have successfully completed the first two Steps, we are now ready to make a decision to rebel or recover. We can continue our hopeless path to a dead end with chemical dependence through use of self-will. Or we can turn our will and our lives over to the care of our Higher Power.

Steps One and Two begin the process of change. Step Three is the action Step. It asks us to do more than change our thinking. It asks us to change our behavior and actively choose recovery.

● How has your behavior been selfish or self-destructive?

_____

_____

_____

_____

● Describe situations when your self-will got you into trouble.

_____

_____

_____

_____

● Do you think that turning your will and life over to a Higher Power may be helpful? _____

Describe why. _____

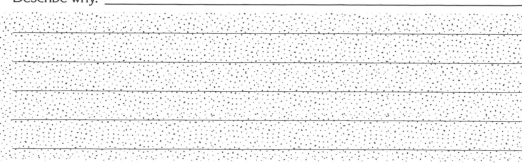

The First Three Steps to Recovery

Here's an easy way to think of what the first three Steps ask us to do:

- Step One asks us to decide whether or not we are chemically dependent.

- Step Two asks us to become willing to change.

- Step Three asks us to act by turning ourselves over to the care of our Higher Power.

the first three Steps

DECIDE

admit we cannot help
ourselves by ourselves

CHANGE

become willing to believe
a Higher Power can help

ACT

turn ourselves over
to a Higher Power

Steps One, Two, and Three take us through a process that helps us admit the problem, confront our need for help, and reach out to get the help we need.

● Describe what you think self-will means.

_____

_____

_____

_____

_____

● Describe what you think turning your life over means.

_____

_____

_____

_____

● How are these two concepts different?

_____

_____

_____

_____

_____

_____

_____

_____

_____

_____

_____

_____

_____

_____

_____

_____

The Feelings List

 here are so many different kinds of feelings we can experience. Often, feelings mix together. Or we may experience two opposing feelings at the same time about a single event. For example, we may feel relieved about being in treatment and, at the same time, feel both afraid and angry.

Here is a list of feelings. Circle the feelings you experience most often. Put an x through those you rarely feel. Add feelings you have that aren't listed.

● Afraid	● Frightened	● Obstinate
● Aggressive	● Frustrated	● Optimistic
● Agonized	● Grievous	● Pained
● Angry	● Guilty	● Paranoid
● Anxious	● Goofy	● Perplexed
● Apologetic	● Ashamed	● Happy
● Regretful	● Bashful	● Hot
● Sad	● Bored	● Hurt
● Shocked	● Cautious	● Hysterical
● Smug	● Cold	● Indifferent
● Sorry	● Confident	● Innocent
● Tense	● Curious	● Jealous
● Disappointed	● Joyful	● Disgusted
● Lonely	● Ecstatic	● Embarrassed
● Lethargic	● Enraged	● Mischievous
● Envious	● Miserable	● Exhausted
● Negative	● _____	● _____
● _____	● _____	● _____

● Look at your list. What feelings are you experiencing right now about being in treatment?

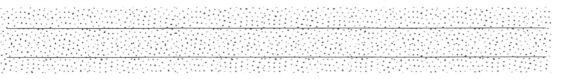

_____

_____

41

Frozen Feelings

Because of your chemical use, you may not have established a healthy way to recognize and accept your own feelings. You also may not have found ways to share feelings with others. Your feelings may seem to be frozen.

Don't think you have to rush out and find your feelings. Identifying, owning, and expressing your feelings in a healthy manner comes naturally as you grow in recovery.

We all go through life in various stages of personal knowledge and acceptance of our feelings. You can start where you are today and grow a little with each new experience.

Experiencing your feelings will bring on a wide range of emotions. But remember, recognizing and accepting your emotions is an important part of your ongoing recovery.

What will he or she think of me?

Anger has never been a problem for me.
I don't get angry at people even when I'd be totally justified.

I should be more understanding.

I never thought my life would turn out like this.

I don't want people to see who I really am.

● Describe a feeling that was frozen before you started your recovery.

_____
_____
_____
_____
_____
_____
_____
_____
_____
_____
_____

● Give examples of feelings you tried to change and how you have tried to change them.

_____
_____
_____
_____
_____
_____
_____
_____
_____
_____
_____

Shame, Grief, Anger, and Fear

Some feelings seem "bigger" than others. The "big" feelings of shame, grief, anger, and fear are especially important for chemically dependent people to recognize as they recover. Sharing these feelings with someone is often the best way to prevent problems that can lead to relapse.

Shame

What Is Shame?

Shame is an inner sense of being basically bad, inadequate, or unworthy. Shame leads to judging yourself and giving yourself a failing grade. Shame often goes hand in hand with addictive behavior. It grows as the addiction grows. Yet, shame is very hard to recognize in ourselves and others.

● What behavior(s) have you identified from your drinking or using that you are ashamed of?

The Effects of Shame

Since shame hides in other emotions, it is hard to spot, particularly in ourselves. Some of our shame messages might sound like this:

- I must not let others know who I really am. I must continue to fool them into believing I am someone that I am not.

- I feel so lonely and isolated inside.

- I am always feeling anxious about everything. That's why I need to stay in control. I can't allow things just to take their course.

- I cannot trust others, because I cannot trust myself. Therefore, I need to manipulate what they think and do.

- I really want to be liked and loved, to be special in other people's eyes. I can only tell whether I'm a good and worthy person by how others react to me.

- I feel like I'm no good.

- What shame messages do you give yourself?

Replacing Shameful Thoughts

Read the following messages over and over. Let them start to replace the shaming messages inside you.

● I can laugh at myself. It's okay to make mistakes; everyone does.

● When I am wrong, I can promptly admit it. I don't need to hide from being human.

● I am a good person. I have unique and special gifts from my Higher Power.

● I can let go of my expectations of other people. I cannot control other people's feelings or behaviors. I am only responsible for me.

● It's okay when people disagree with me or act as if they don't like me. I know I'm okay.

● Write the messages you will begin to give yourself to replace your shaming messages.

Grief

As we change our lifestyle from chemical use to abstinence and recovery, we can experience grief because of the loss of the relationship we've had with chemicals.

In addition to grieving the loss of our chemical, we can also grieve over other losses. Many of these losses may be attributed to our chemical use. Here are some examples:

- Loss of a loved one
- Loss of a home
- Loss of a marriage or relationship
- Loss of a contract
- Loss of physical abilities

- Loss of a pet
- Loss of a job
- Loss of a co-worker or friend
- Loss of good health
- Loss of a possession with sentimental value

The greater the loss is to us, the greater the grief. When we experience loss, grief is the normal and healthy way to respond. We can handle grief by accepting it as an honest emotion. Turning to our Higher Power, attending self-help meetings, using the Twelve Steps of Alcoholics Anonymous, and talking with friends all help us work through our grief. By naming and working through our feelings of grief we can reach the peace and serenity we deserve.

- List the losses you have experienced that happened as a result of your chemical use.

Anger

Anger is a complex emotion. Some people use anger to cover up other feelings. Some cover up their anger with feelings of sadness or by laughing it off. Do you express angry feelings? Or cover them up and stuff them inside of you?

Being angry affects the tone in our voices, the way we walk, our posture, and our gestures and expressions. Anger can block us from feeling good about ourselves and from sharing that goodness with others. If we let anger turn into resentment that controls our thoughts and behavior, we will not fully experience the benefits offered in recovery.

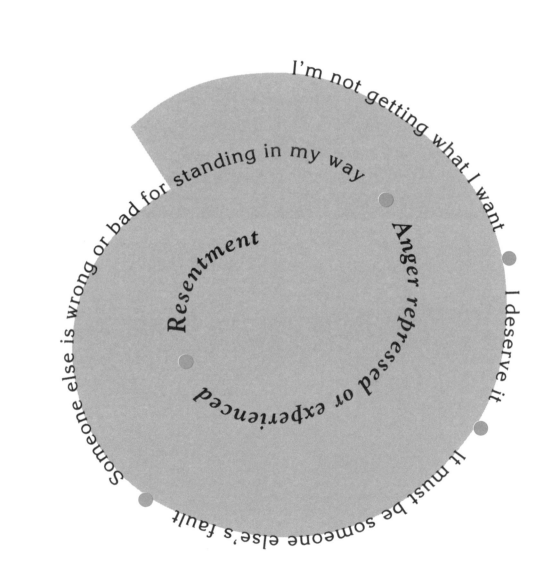

I'm not getting what I want

Someone else is wrong or bad for standing in my way

Resentment

Anger repressed or experienced

I deserve it

It must be someone else's fault

Anger often follows a pattern that starts with self-will and ends in resentment.

48

● Describe how you show others you are angry.

● How did your use of alcohol or other drugs help you cover up angry feelings?

Fear

Fear is a feeling that is common to all people, especially to those who are chemically dependent. Often, alcohol and other drugs are used to hide from fearful situations or nagging anxiety. The secrets and lies that surround the abuse of mind-altering chemicals can cause fear to play a major role in our lives.

Often, fear freezes us. It prevents us from taking action while it continues to grow. In time, fear and anxiety become so common that both feelings are always present without any particular reason.

Many recovering people have found that, as their lives gradually move toward a base of honesty and spirituality, their feelings of constant dread disappear. However, in early recovery the fear of living without the use of chemicals can be great. Also, while using chemicals, our behavior may have created many immediate problems. To face such challenges sober can be very frightening.

● Describe one part of your life today that makes you afraid.

_____

_____

_____

_____

_____

_____

● What are you afraid of now while in treatment?

_____

_____

_____

_____

_____

_____

Identify, Own, Accept, and Share

Experiencing feelings more fully is new and strange to most of us. We can take some steps to help us in this new process:

Identify: What am I feeling? In the past, we either denied our feelings or acted them out in inappropriate ways. Now we slow down and identify or name what we are feeling — angry, glad, sad, afraid, ashamed, hurt, etc.

Own: If we did name a feeling, rarely did we own it as our own. Instead, we reacted and blamed others: You make me angry; you hurt me, and so on. The feeling is ours. So is the response or behavior we choose: I'm angry; I'm afraid; I'm happy.

Accept: Feelings are a part of us — they just are. We don't have to deny them or judge them, just accept them as okay. We all have feelings. And we all have choices about how to respond to them: I accept this feeling as real.

Share: We have kept our feelings secret. We attempted to deny, control, or change our feelings by using alcohol or other drugs. Feelings have energy. And they can become like a pressure cooker. Sharing with our group or sponsor is a way to express these feelings in a healthy manner. Sharing keeps the pressure from building up, keeps us from isolating ourselves, and helps us to "let go."

Some Facts About Feelings

Feelings follow change: Feelings often come about when changes are taking place. When you re-think, re-do, re-organize or re-arrange, feelings just happen.

Feelings arise from our relationships with others: Feelings come in relationships with other people—parents, spouse or partner, boss, children, neighbors, friend—anyone with whom you communicate.

Feelings don't just disappear: If feelings are ignored, they don't just go away. Feelings stick around and take other shapes and forms. For example, feelings can become an attitude: instead of feeling angry, I can become an angry person. If ignored, feelings often damage your physical or mental health.

Feelings can be sneaky: Often your feelings come in disguises. You can mislabel your emotions. For example, you can feel you are angry when you are really afraid. You can feel confused when you are really angry.

Feelings can lead to relapse: If you do not learn to accept and express your feelings honestly and appropriately, you can be tempted to use the ineffective and damaging alternative of chemical use.

Feelings just are: Feelings, by themselves, are not wrong or right. They just are a part of you.

Feelings can change: No matter how strong they may be at first, feelings can change.

Path to Recovery

Making Wise Choices

 ou want to stay sober. You want to experience the promises of a serene life. Many people who leave treatment have good intentions. But the cunning, baffling, and powerful nature of the disease of chemical dependence causes them to use chemicals again.

Many things happen that can cause a relapse. If you regularly note the signs that indicate you might be close to relapse, you can avoid it. For example, if you find that you are slacking off on some of the activities listed on page 54, be aware that you may be toying with relapse. If you work at recovery, you can prevent the dangers of relapse from occurring in the first place.

The path to recovery is different for each of us. But we all share a common need to work on every aspect of our lives, including the physical, social, psychological, and spiritual. When we detect signs that something is "off" in our recovery program, we can stop, identify, own, accept, and share that problem or feeling. For example, if we feel stressed, we can explore it and take appropriate action. Or if we often find excuses to avoid meetings, we may talk that through with a sponsor and seek support from others to get to our meetings at least weekly.

Remember to use all your recovery tools. Meetings, sponsors, friends, phone calls and attention to healthy sleeping, eating, and exercise patterns can help. On the next page are some resources that can help you in recovery. Circle those you think will be particularly helpful and add to the list.

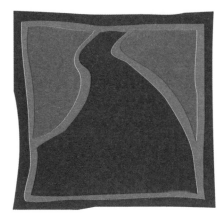

The Path to Recovery

Attend AA
or NA meetings

Share in meetings

Find a sponsor

Remain honest

Listen to others

Admit mistakes

Remain patient

Attend aftercare

Eat regular meals

Share angry feelings
appropriately

Tell your story

Get adequate rest

Affirm your
worth daily

Connect with others

Work at letting go

Say the
Serenity Prayer

Meditate daily

Talk to others

Be active

Share

Think positively

Live one day at a time

Stay in the present

Confront fears

Schedule wisely

Be assertive

Laugh

Allow time for fun

Resolve
financial/legal
problems

Talk about negative
thoughts or feelings

Keep in touch with
your Higher Power

Recovery Plan

Planning our recovery is essential work to be done before we leave a structured recovery program. With our plan in hand, we are better prepared to lay a good foundation to be and stay sober and recover.

The pathway to relapse or recovery.

SELF-WILL

The Pathway to Relapse

Unhealthy

"I pledge to change."

Self-will

"I can beat this."

Dry Period

"I am strong."

Relapse Behavior

"I can do it myself."

ACCEPTANCE

The Pathway to Recovery

Healthy

"I am powerless over chemicals."

Acceptance

"I give up."

Serenity/Sobriety

"I surrender."

● Meetings are the foundation of AA and NA. How many AA or NA meetings will you attend? Location, day, time?

_____

_____

_____

_____

● Sponsorship is an important part of AA and NA. How will you find an AA or NA sponsor?

_____

_____

_____

_____

● In the past, in what situations were you most likely to use alcohol or other drugs? When you face these situations now, what will you do instead?

_____

_____

_____

_____

● What actions will you take when you get angry or frustrated?

_____

_____

_____

_____

● How will you start each day? End each day?

● What are some actions you can take when you are lonely?

● What are some actions you can take when you are not getting along with friends or family?

● What are some actions you can take if the meetings you're attending begin to feel boring or unimportant?

● What plans do you have to eat and rest properly? To exercise regularly?

_____

_____

_____

_____

● Describe how you will handle situations that make you feel afraid.

_____

_____

_____

_____

_____

● What life events or losses could cause you to drink or use other drugs?

_____

_____

_____

_____

_____

● What will you do or whom will you turn to if any of these events occur?

_____

_____

_____

_____

_____

● Make a list of people who can give you positive support in times of need.

● Will you be able to ask these people for help? Describe how you will do so.

● Describe chemical-free activities you will take part in just for fun or relaxation.

The Path Ahead

You have worked through the first three Steps of Alcoholics Anonymous, and you have done a great deal of work toward recovery and healing. You have also worked on important problems like denial, powerlessness, and unmanageability. You have thought through your feelings, both in what they are and how you handle them. Perhaps most important of all, you have developed a plan of action to help you live differently, to live free of the nightmare of chemical dependence.

The remaining Steps in the Alcoholics Anonymous program provide you with the tools to continue building a strong foundation of recovery. Your work is not done just yet. Steps Four and Five will help you take an inventory of your life thus far and talk that through with another human being. The rest of this workbook—which focuses on Steps Four and Five—will show you how to do that. Steps Six through Twelve will help you maintain healthy recovery by keeping yourself in check, sharing what you know with others, and nurturing your spiritual connections.

You have already done some important work toward recovery. The path ahead of you now leads to a better way of living.

Work hard, ask for help, and enjoy recovery!

Introduction to Steps Four and Five

The Twelve Steps of Alcoholics Anonymous lay out a path to chemical-free and sober living. Our recovery path of contented sobriety begins each day with the first three Steps. With every step on our recovery path, we are provided tools to help us maintain our sobriety: the Serenity Prayer, the Twelve Steps, slogans, sponsors, meetings, support groups, spirituality, friends, the telephone, and so on. Steps One, Two, and Three take us through a process that helps us admit the problem, acknowledge our need for help, and reach out to get that help. Once we have taken those first three Steps, we are ready to further strengthen our foundation by taking Steps Four and Five. For many of us in recovery, these two Steps are not easy. However, if we make them honestly and thoroughly, they provide great healing.

Over the next few pages, you will find a number of character traits (ways of thinking/behaving) listed. Some are negative; some are positive. Each negative trait is paired with its corresponding positive trait. Begin your inventory by looking over all the negative traits first. Then, answer the questions that follow each one as honestly as possible.

After taking an inventory of your negative traits, go back and look carefully at the positive traits that are paired with them. Answer the questions that follow each of the positive traits as honestly as possible. Note that under the positive traits, you will have a chance to set some goals to help you continue along your recovery path. Be specific and thorough, but move along at your own pace. Remember, this is your recovery path, no one else's.

Taking an honest look at ourselves can be frightening. We will need courage to be open to our unresolved or frozen feelings. Our courage will also help us be open to memories that cause us guilt, shame, fear, or resentment. Know that it's important for you to take that look. If you begin to feel uncomfortable, don't give up. Instead, turn to the first Three Steps or any of the tools that have helped you fashion your recovery so far. For example, you can let your sponsor or your group know that you're beginning to work on your Fourth Step inventory. This recovery path may be yours, but your sponsor and group—and many others—have walked it before you and are walking it with you now. You are not alone, and you don't have to take this Step alone.

Made a searching and fearless moral inventory of ourselves.

Self-Honesty

In the past, our chemical use prevented us from really seeing ourselves. So, working on Step Four may be the first chance we've had in a long time to view ourselves honestly. Step Four helps us look at our whole life, not just our behavior when we were actively using chemicals. Taking Step Four, then, is not just looking at the bad things we've done, but at our talents and good qualities as well. Looking at where we have been will help us to move forward. It will help us to look at who we are and see who we can become.

Therefore, as we prepare our inventory, we will look at our character traits—both positive and negative. Positive behaviors are called our strengths. Negative behaviors are our weaknesses. In the past, both types of behavior have provided us protection by supporting our denial—denial of how chemicals have affected our lives and the lives of those around us. To view ourselves more openly and honestly, we need to strip away these "protective" layers of denial one by one. The Fourth Step inventory will help us do just that.

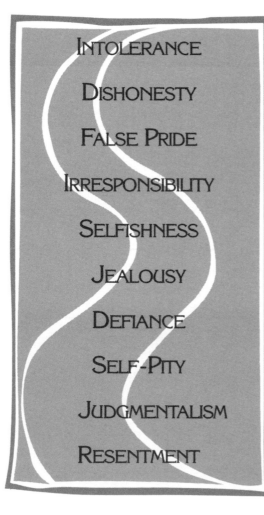

INTOLERANCE

DISHONESTY

FALSE PRIDE

IRRESPONSIBILITY

SELFISHNESS

JEALOUSY

DEFIANCE

SELF-PITY

JUDGMENTALISM

RESENTMENT

TOLERANCE

HONESTY

MODESTY

RESPONSIBILITY

SHARING

TRUST

COOPERATION

SELF-WORTH

EMPATHY

FORGIVENESS

Intolerance

As chemically dependent people, we often were intolerant of others' beliefs, feelings, or values. Our thinking said, "My way is the only way." We showed our intolerance through discrimination (sexual, racial), biased thinking, or prejudiced actions.

● Ways I have been intolerant:

_____

_____

_____

_____

_____

_____

_____

● My intolerant thinking and acting have resulted in the following:

_____

_____

_____

_____

_____

_____

_____

_____

_____

Tolerance

As we begin to learn more about ourselves, we feel less threatened by others' opinions, values, and beliefs. We learn that there is more than one way to accomplish the same thing. Once we become more confident in who we are and in what we believe, we can be more accepting of others' ideas.

● Ways I can be more tolerant are:

_____

_____

_____

_____

_____

_____

_____

● The result of this new behavior will be:

_____

_____

_____

_____

_____

● My goals to become even more tolerant are:

_____

_____

_____

_____

_____

_____

Dishonesty

Many times we were dishonest with ourselves, family, friends, and business associates in order to cover up our mistakes caused by our chemical use. We acted with dishonesty through our deceitful behavior, lies, minimizing, exaggerating, and cheating.

● Examples of how I have been dishonest are:

_____

_____

_____

_____

_____

_____

_____

_____

● My dishonest thinking and acting have resulted in the following:

_____

_____

_____

_____

_____

_____

_____

_____

_____

_____

_____

Honesty

The very first Step on the path to recovery was to become honest with ourselves. Having made that Step, we can now begin to be honest with others. We can show this in our behavior by acting in ways that are sincere, frank, and truthful.

● Steps I have taken to become more honest are:

_____

_____

_____

_____

_____

_____

● The results of this behavior have been:

_____

_____

_____

_____

_____

_____

_____

● My goals to become even more honest are:

_____

_____

_____

_____

_____

_____

False Pride

When we were actively using alcohol or other drugs, we believed we were "oh, so important," often at the expense of others. We were showoffs, imposing, and very self-centered.

● Some examples of my false pride are:

_____

_____

_____

_____

_____

_____

_____

My prideful thinking and acting have resulted in the following:

_____

_____

_____

_____

_____

_____

_____

_____

_____

_____

Modesty

In recovery, we begin to like ourselves again. We become more accepting of our strengths and limitations and no longer need to hide behind obnoxious behavior to justify our self-worth.

● Ways I have tried to become more accepting of who I am are:

_____
_____
_____
_____
_____

● The results of this new behavior have been:

_____
_____
_____
_____
_____

● My goals to become even more accepting and modest are:

_____
_____
_____
_____
_____
_____

Irresponsibility

Irresponsible behavior can show itself in a variety of ways. Perhaps we were irresponsible in our relationship with family, friends, employers, and creditors. Or maybe we were irresponsible in taking care of ourselves, neglecting our basic needs. Anytime we were immature, reckless, neglectful, or impulsive we were being irresponsible.

● Examples of how I have been irresponsible are:

_____

_____

_____

_____

_____

_____

_____

● My irresponsible thinking and acting have resulted in the following:

_____

_____

_____

_____

_____

_____

_____

_____

_____

_____

_____

Responsibility

On our recovery path, we begin to accept responsibility for ourselves. The more we accept and own our actions, thoughts, behaviors, and feelings, the better we feel about ourselves.

● I am becoming more responsible by:

● The results of this new behavior have been:

● My goals to become even more responsible are:

Selfishness

In the past, we were selfish and self-centered. We thought only of our own desires and wants, and would become upset if anything interfered with them. Most of the time this was at the expense of others. We became demanding, self-centered, and controlling.

● Examples of my selfish behavior:

_____

_____

_____

_____

_____

_____

_____

● My selfish thinking and acting have resulted in the following:

_____

_____

_____

_____

_____

_____

_____

_____

_____

_____

_____

Sharing

As we have moved along our recovery path, we have learned more about sharing: sharing our experiences with others, sharing ourselves, sharing our time.

● Ways I have begun to share more of myself:

_____

_____

_____

_____

_____

_____

_____

● The results of this new behavior have been:

_____

_____

_____

_____

_____

_____

● My goals to share even more include:

_____

_____

_____

_____

_____

_____

_____

Jealousy

Many negative behaviors overlap one another. Jealousy results from our self-centeredness and mistrust. If we are insecure with ourselves, we will believe that we must be the center of our loved ones' attention. We tend to believe that if our loved ones like someone else, they must not like us. This is jealousy, and jealousy has caused us and others much grief.

● My jealous behaviors include:

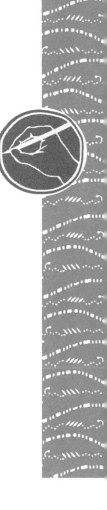

_____

_____

_____

_____

_____

_____

_____

● My jealous thinking and acting have resulted in the following:

_____

_____

_____

_____

_____

_____

_____

_____

_____

Trust

In recovery, we begin to trust ourselves more. As we do this, we will also develop trust and confidence in others.

● Ways I have begun to trust others are:

_____

_____

_____

_____

_____

_____

● The results of this new behavior have been:

_____

_____

_____

_____

_____

_____

● My goals to become even more trusting are:

_____

_____

_____

_____

_____

Defiance

We have challenged or disobeyed anyone or anything that we viewed as a threat. Many times our perceptions were unfounded.

● These are examples of how I defied or disobeyed:

_____

_____

_____

_____

_____

_____

_____

● My defiant and disobedient thinking and acting have resulted in the following:

_____

_____

_____

_____

_____

_____

_____

_____

_____

_____

_____

Cooperation

Our recovery program teaches us cooperation. All of us in our support group work together for contented and continued sobriety.

● I am showing cooperation by:

_____
_____
_____
_____
_____
_____
_____

● The results of this behavior have been:

_____
_____
_____
_____
_____
_____
_____

● My goals to become even more cooperative are:

_____
_____
_____
_____
_____
_____
_____

Self-Pity

We have been pros at feeling sorry for ourselves. We were experts of the victim game, with our "If only they understood me," and "If only they would get off my back," and "Woe is me!" No matter what happened, it was always someone else's fault.

● These are examples of how I felt sorry for myself:

_____
_____
_____
_____
_____
_____
_____

● My self-pitying thoughts and actions have resulted in the following:

_____
_____
_____
_____
_____
_____
_____
_____
_____
_____

Self-Worth

As we begin to recognize and develop our positive characteristics, we assume more responsibility for our actions and our lives. We acknowledge our limitations and recognize our strengths. We begin to experience and believe in our own self-worth.

● I show that I believe in my self-worth by:

_____

_____

_____

_____

_____

_____

● The results of this new behavior have been:

_____

_____

_____

_____

_____

_____

● My goals to enhance my self-worth are:

_____

_____

_____

_____

_____

Judgmentalism

We had opinions on or about anyone and anything. We displayed judgmental behavior in our rigid, black and white attitudes. Our stance was, "I'm right and you're wrong." We believed we could correct the seeming injustices of the world, community, and friends.

● These are examples of how I have been judgmental:

_____
_____
_____
_____
_____
_____
_____

● My judgmental thinking and acting have resulted in the following:

_____
_____
_____
_____
_____
_____
_____
_____
_____
_____
_____

Empathy

When we try to understand another's point of view or feelings, we empathize with that person. We don't necessarily have to agree with the other person, but empathy can provide understanding and enhance our relationship with him or her.

●   This is how I am trying to become more empathetic and accepting:

_____

_____

_____

_____

_____

_____

●   The results of this behavior have been:

_____

_____

_____

_____

_____

_____

●   My goals to become even more empathetic and accepting are:

_____

_____

_____

_____

_____

_____

Resentment

Resentment means holding fast to a feeling that someone's done us wrong. We cling tightly to what we believe has hurt us. We feel the slight over and over again until it begins to affect our behavior. We become angry and revengeful. We are no longer in control of our feeling of resentment: it controls us. Resentment clouds our thoughts and actions.

● Resentments that I have held on to are:

_____

_____

_____

_____

_____

_____

_____

● My resentful thinking and acting have resulted in the following:

_____

_____

_____

_____

_____

_____

_____

_____

_____

_____

_____

Forgiveness

As the positive traits of tolerance, acceptance, honesty, trust, and self-worth develop, we will be able to overcome resentment with forgiveness. But first, we need to forgive ourselves. After we have done this, we will be able to forgive others and to receive their forgiveness as well.

● I have forgiven myself for:

_____

_____

_____

_____

_____

● I have forgiven others for:

_____

_____

_____

_____

_____

● The results of this behavior have included the following:

_____

_____

_____

_____

● Areas in which I need to continue forgiving myself are:

● Areas in which I need to continue forgiving others are:

Admitted

to God, to

ourselves

and to

another

human being

the exact

nature of our

wrongs.

Self-Disclosure

Now that we've completed our Fourth Step inventory, our next step is to share it. The Fifth Step asks us to share the information we have discovered in our inventory with God, ourselves, and another human being.

While working on our Fourth Step inventory, we begin to admit our behavior to ourselves. Sharing with God allows us to own up to our behavior. Sharing with another human being helps us strip away even more layers of denial that have shielded us from interacting with others. Overall, the Fifth Step takes us further down our recovery path and out from under the dark clouds of isolation, fear, and guilt. Use these guidelines to work your Fifth Step:

1. Find someone you believe you can trust and who understands the Twelve Steps of Alcoholics Anonymous.

2. Reread Chapters 5 and 6 in *Alcoholics Anonymous*.

3. Meet in a quiet place that has minimal distractions.

4. Allow yourself sufficient time to complete the Fifth Step. Be thorough and specific; do not rush through it.

5. Remember confidentiality, not only in what you share but also in what your Fifth Step partner may share with you.

Once you have completed the Fifth Step, allow yourself some quiet time to focus on where you are now on your journey. Realize that you may or may not "feel" different once you have finished the Fifth Step. But also realize that how you feel at this point is not as important as how open and willing you are to change as you continue along your recovery path.

Finding a Fifth Step Partner

Sharing our Fifth Step with another human being helps us remain honest in what we share about ourselves. It also gives us the chance to see ourselves as we are — both the good and the bad. When we embrace our good points, we build our self-esteem. When we admit our flawed points, we join the rest of the human race: we acknowledge that we aren't perfect. Exploring both sides helps us know ourselves; that knowledge strengthens all aspects of our recovery process.

But many of us have never learned to trust others. Choosing a Fifth Step partner is a first step toward reaching out and letting others help. It's also a step toward trusting another human being with our secrets, our lives.

If we take a moment to simply imagine with whom we might be comfortable sharing our Fifth Step, our inner selves will often guide the selection. For example, we can spend some quiet moments thinking back about who we trusted or felt safe with in our past lives. A clergy person? A friend or a group of friends? A relative?

Carefully consider many people before making your choice: clergy, aftercare counselor, sponsor, AA group, or friend. Some people are trained to hear Fifth Steps and can be located by contacting a treatment center or aftercare program. And carefully assess your own needs: are you most comfortable with women? men? people of a particular culture, race, or ethnic group?

● Write down the name of one or two people with whom you would feel comfortable giving your Fifth Step:

_____

_____

● List some of the things you fear in sharing your Fifth Step with another person:

_____

_____

_____

_____

_____

_____

● List some of the good things you think may happen by sharing your Fifth Step with someone else:

_____

_____

_____

_____

_____

_____

_____

_____

Preparing for the Fifth Step

You can best prepare for taking a Fifth Step by:

- reading and meditating, specifically by reviewing chapters 5 and 6 in *Alcoholics Anonymous* (the *Big Book*);

- writing out a Fourth Step inventory in advance, to use as a guide during the Fifth Step; and

- carefully selecting the time and place so you have both a comfortable, safe, and confidential place in which to talk through the Fifth Step, as well as enough time to do it in an unhurried, thoughtful way.

There is no right way to give a Fifth Step. It can be done in a restaurant or church or apartment or group meeting room. It can be done during a walk or while sitting on a park bench. The time, the place, and the person should be chosen thoughtfully. The goal is to give a Fifth Step in as clear and honest a way as possible. We can all do this best by clearing away distractions. That means advance attention paid to who, what, and where.

- In what setting will you feel most comfortable?

_____

_____

_____

_____

_____

- What arrangements will you need to make to determine who, what, and where?

_____

_____

_____

_____

_____

● What do you want most to accomplish in giving your Fifth Step?

_____

_____

_____

_____

_____

_____

_____

_____

_____

_____

_____

_____

_____

_____

_____

_____

Taking the Fifth Step

Again, there is no right way to take a Fifth Step. When you are ready, simply start at the beginning. You can either talk freely or use your Fourth Step inventory to guide you. The listener will simply listen. The time is yours to peel back the layers and reveal what lies below. Your goal is to voice who and what you are, what you have been and done.

By concentrating on the process of saying your inventory, you can avoid pitfalls like: worrying about what the listener is thinking; tempering how things come out; or altering words in any way to soften or tone the meaning or implication. This is your Fifth Step, to be told as directly and honestly as you can. Choosing words carefully is not necessary. You are not engaged in this activity in order to impress anyone else.

There is little value in making things sound better or nicer. By speaking the truth, you will hear the truth. By hearing the truth, you will know yourself better than you ever have. And that knowledge is the foundation of recovery — knowing what you need will help you take steps to change and nurture yourself.

- How do you feel about taking the Fifth Step? Do you still have some fears about it? What are they?

- What can you do to calm these fears before you take the Step?

- Do you harbor any negative feelings or attitudes about taking the Fifth Step that may interfere with doing it successfully?

● What can you do to nurture a positive attitude going into your Fifth Step?

_____

_____

_____

_____

_____

What to Expect After Taking the Fifth Step

Some people throw a party; some people ceremonially burn their Fourth Step inventory; some people spend time alone or with others processing the experience. Whether you celebrate or contemplate, expect a range of feelings that, at times, may conflict with each other.

You may feel happy and sad at the same time: happy you've accomplished this Fifth Step, but sad at some of the things you revealed in it. You may feel guilt over things you did, but real pride in preparing and giving a good, honest Fifth Step. Hopefully, the overriding feeling will be one of relief, of feeling better, of feeling lighter.

How you feel will depend on the expectations you have set ahead of time. Try to avoid either under or overestimating the outcome. Know that it will be rewarding if done as honestly as possible. Expect a positive result, but don't be alarmed if you don't experience a miracle of some sort.

When finished, reward yourself in a healthy way for what you have done. Completing a Fifth Step is a major accomplishment. It demonstrates a willingness on your part to accept the AA program of recovery into your life. And it shows that you are willing to work hard to remain abstinent, to do what it takes to heal.

● How do you expect to feel after completing the Fifth Step?

_____

_____

_____

_____

● How will you take time to reward or think about your Fifth Step experience when you finish?

_____

_____

_____

_____

_____

_____

_____

_____

Continuing the Journey

The knowledge revealed in Steps Four and Five helps us understand the defects and strengths we take with us into recovery. This knowledge can become an important road map that guides what we do to remain abstinent and happy in our recovery. And, sharing the Fifth Step with another person is often the little encouragement or nudge we need to start trusting others again. That trust helps us ask for and accept needed care and advice from those around us. We can rely on many sources beyond ourselves to change, grow, and share the struggles and triumphs of our recovery process.

Steps Six through Twelve offer us further involvement in a way of recovery that will help us remain abstinent and happy. By coming this far in your recovery, you have built a strong foundation. You have the tools of recovery in hand, and the plan laid out before you. You can continue building your recovery one day at a time, one step at a time.

NOTES

NOTES

NOTES

NOTES